HURRICANE HAZEL

For Eleanor

HURRICANE HAZEL

Canada's Storm of the Century

Jim Gifford

THE DUNDURN GROUP
TORONTO

Copy-Editor: Andrea Pruss
Design: Jennifer Scott
Printer: Friesens

National Library of Canada Cataloguing in Publication Data

Gifford, Jim
    Hurricane Hazel : Canada's storm of the century / Jim Gifford.

Includes bibliographical references.
ISBN 1-55002-526-0

1. Hurricane Hazel, l954. I. Title.

QC959.C3G53 2004   363.34'922'09713   C2004-903137-6

1   2   3   4   5   08   07   06   05   04

Canadä

We acknowledge the support of the **Canada Council for the Arts** and the **Ontario Arts Council** for our publishing program. We also acknowledge the financial support of the **Government of Canada** through the **Book Publishing Industry Development Program** and **The Association for the Export of Canadian Books**, and the **Government of Ontario** through the **Ontario Book Publishers Tax Credit** program, and the **Ontario Media Development Corporation**'s **Ontario Book Initiative**.

Care has been taken to trace the ownership of copyright material used in this book. The author and the publisher welcome any information enabling them to rectify any references or credit in subsequent editions.

J. Kirk Howard, President

Printed and bound in Canada.
Printed on recycled paper.
www.dundurn.com

Dundurn Press
8 Market Street
Suite 200
Toronto, Ontario, Canada
M5E 1M6

Gazelle Book Services Limited
White Cross Mills
Hightown, Lancaster, England
LA1 4X5

Dundurn Press
2250 Military Road
Tonawanda NY
U.S.A. 14150

FOREWORD

BY MIKE FILEY

THE YEAR WAS 1954; THE DATE, OCTOBER 15; the weather, wet … boy was it wet! Back then I was still just a kid. Well, to be absolutely honest, I had graduated from "kid" to "teenager" just four days earlier. I was living in the family home on Elvina Gardens in North Toronto, and as strange as this may seem, the idea that a hurricane might be approaching the city was totally absurd. Sure there had been mention of Hazel in the previous days' newspapers, but hurricanes only happened south of the border … didn't they? On that special Friday there had been a lot of rain, but what the heck, there'd been lots of rain that entire week. But now, as I made my way home from school, it seemed as if the rain was coming down even harder.

Thinking back a half-century, the idea that a hurricane might be headed our way wasn't even mentioned on the city's one television station (CBLT, Channel 9) or on any of the local radio newscasts. At 4:00 P.M. I began my afternoon delivery job at the late Pat Higgins's place, Mount Pleasant Fish and Chips, where, if it wasn't busy, I would scrub and peel potatoes. This being a Friday night (and with certain religious beliefs still very much in place) there wasn't time for that. All of my time would be spent delivering either halibut and chips (at thirty cents an order) or haddock and chips (same chips, different fish, twenty-five cents an order).

The shop wasn't far from the corner of Broadway Avenue and Mount Pleasant Road, where the pair of streets met in a minor hollow. As the afternoon turned into evening, that hollow began to fill with water so that by six or seven o'clock, as I wheeled my bike through the intersection to deliver orders on the other side of Mount Pleasant, water would come in over the top of my boots. This was some deluge. The day ended and I went to bed, rain still pelting the windows of my bedroom. And still I hadn't heard the word "hurricane." And, in fact, didn't until the following morning, when all of the country learned that this witch called Hurricane Hazel had caused such great loss of life and inflicted tremendous damage to the north and west of the city.

I felt bad that while all of this was going on, my main concern was getting those fish and chip orders through.

MIKE FILEY

ACKNOWLEDGEMENTS

I MUST FIRST EXPRESS MY GRATITUDE TO THE crew at Dundurn Press: Kirk Howard, Beth Bruder, Tony Hawke, Barry Jowett, Andrea Pruss, Jennifer Scott, and Anna Synenko. Dundurn has published many excellent books on Toronto history over the years, and for that reason they were the only publisher I approached with the idea for this project.

It did not prove easy to gather first-hand accounts and photographs of the aftermath of Hurricane Hazel. Without the participation of those I interviewed and those who trusted me with their photographs I would never have been able to complete this book. Many welcomed me into their living rooms, met me at Tim Hortons, found time for a lengthy phone call, or suffered my flurries of e-mails, including Don Boyd, Al Brierley, Harry Bruce, Michael Campbell, Jack Carson, Nick Chometa, Jim Crawford, Byard Donnelly, Stan Elphick, Peter Ferguson, Mike Filey, Edith George, Ken Gibbs, David Imrie, Dave Iris, Hans Kotiessen, Helen Lee, Don Leslie, Hazel McCallion, Tudi Nuttley, Frank Orr, Wayne Plunkett, Roman

Tarnovetsky, Mary Jane Thorne-Rees, John Thurston, Norma Vineham, Joyce Walker, and Neil Walker.

For generous donations of photographs or assistance in finding them I thank Don Haley, Rosemary Hasner, and Deanne Rodrigue of the Toronto and Region Conservation Authority; Heather McKinnon of the Lake Simcoe Region Conservation Authority; Jeanne Andrews of Environment Canada; Major Ira E. Barrow and Karl Larson of the Salvation Army Museum; Lloyd Cully; Bill Dixon; Martin Taylor; Steven Elphick; John Elphick; Richard Sargent; Beth Tokawa, formerly of the Toronto Port Authority; Thomas E. Allan, St. John Ambulance; Vinitha Pathmarajah, YWCA; Alan Walker, Toronto Reference Library; and Sean Smith of the York University Archives. I also thank the City of Toronto Archives, the Archives of Ontario, the National Archives of Canada, and the Toronto Police Museum for their contributions to this project.

I must single out Paula Elphick, Eva Ferguson, Marj Mossman, Mary Louise Ashbourne, Tina Hardt, and the other members of the Weston Historical Society for trusting me with their precious records and for allowing me a forum to meet their members, many of whom witnessed Hazel's wrath in Weston and Etobicoke.

I thank Beth Crane for her technical advice and for otherwise seeing me through the storm.

For their continued support over the years, I thank my brother, Glen Gifford; Ken and Pat Wright; Michael Wright; Mark Wright; David Bolter, Nancie Im-Bolter, and wee Gwyneth Bolter; Geoff and Mary Bolter; Bill Harvey; John and Liza Harvey; Adrienne Leahey; Craig MacInnis; Steve Beattie; Ted Barris; Aaron Adel; Sarah Williams; Patrick Crean; Alyssa Stuart; Jim Allen; Howard Hewer; Barbara Jones; and my walking partners, Bella and Joe. I mustn't forget Steve Bevan, Dean Towers, Andrew Goodman, J. Bettis, and the others who for so long have met me at the confluence.

Special thanks to Mike Filey, who took time away from his busy schedule to write a foreword to this book.

Thank you, Maria. You have been with me nearly half my life. I can't imagine what my world would be like without you.

Finally, to my mom, Eleanor, who first told me about Hurricane Hazel: I love you and miss you and wish you were here to see this.

JIM GIFFORD

HURRICANE HAZEL

IN October 1954, Toronto was a small town. The population had crept up to over a million inhabitants, and families trucked in from across Canada and around the world. Industry boomed. New streets lined with new houses sprouted up everywhere, revitalizing the sleepy suburbs that wrapped around the city's core, connecting them. But for all its growth, Toronto was still a small town.

Long before the CN Tower loomed over the skyline, Toronto was a city of independent neighbourhoods and communities: East York, Weston, Willowdale, Leaside, Don Mills, Royal York, Humber Summit, Lansing, Long Branch, Swansea. Now they have all been swallowed up by amalgamation; the names remaining on road signs identify what were once small villages nestled within a cosmopolitan collective.

In 1954 people knew their neighbours. In the summer, they talked over their back fences and shouted greetings across the street over the squeals of children playing. It was a time when neighbours really did drop by for a cup of sugar, and when someone needed help with something, you gave it.

The Yonge subway line had opened in March of that year. Passengers rattled along, one arm gripping a strap for balance, the other holding a folded *Toronto Telegram*, or perhaps the *Toronto Daily Star*, as they journeyed to their jobs at Eaton's at Yonge and College or at the banks farther south or in the growing number of specialty shops and businesses. Television was just becoming affordable for many. When the Toronto Argonauts played against the Ottawa Rough Riders in the first televised football game in Canada in September, most viewers were treated to their first Canadian Football League game. But when Marilyn Bell swam successfully across Lake Ontario, most still heard about it on the radio or read about it in the newspaper.

In Canada the weather makes up much of the news, especially in Toronto, where any major change in the forecast becomes a front-page story. Most often, Toronto's weather is unremarkable: moderate summers with a few blistering days; moderate winters with a few heavy snowfalls. The autumns are cool and dry, for many the favourite time of year. Rarely does

Martin Taylor

As if in a dream, pavement appears to float near the Lawrence Avenue bridge dividing Etobicoke and Weston. For many, Hurricane Hazel was a surreal experience far removed from the routine of daily life. Martin Taylor was among dozens of engineering students at the University of Toronto who searched the Humber River for bodies after the storm. "Each engineering student was expected to walk the Humber," he recalls. Taylor ventured out from his home near Church Street and Jane Avenue the day after the storm to photograph the destruction.

the city see severe conditions, and when it does the novelty becomes, for some, a reason to celebrate.

Nobody celebrated the weather on the night of October 15, 1954. Later, people would celebrate the heroes of Hurricane Hazel: the men who rowed the streets of flooded neighbourhoods looking for survivors stranded on rooftops;

Above left: *Curiosity seekers on the Etobicoke side of the Lawrence Avenue bridge look over into Weston. Police monitored the deteriorating situation and closed the bridge shortly before its middle section was washed away.*

Above right: *Onlookers on the Weston side of the Lawrence Avenue bridge.*

the volunteers who kept the coffee pots gurgling and the sandwiches coming as the rescuers went out once again, hoping that that family was still clinging to the roof of the house at the end of the street; and the firemen, Boy Scouts, and other conscripts who spent long days away from their families when the water receded, walking river valleys looking for bodies.

In only twenty-four hours in October 1954, more than eight inches of rain — millions of gallons of water — fell on the Humber River watershed alone. Toronto saw its worst flooding in two hundred years. Nearly four thousand families were left

Surveying the damage along the shores of the Humber River in Etobicoke. At the turn of the millennium, Maclean's magazine ranked Hurricane Hazel as one of the top fifty nation-building events of the twentieth century.

Gordon W. Powley/Archives of Ontario/E 5-2-2-22-1/10002913

homeless, and eighty-one people lost their lives. Many more would have been lost were it not for the efforts of dozens of brave men and women, some of whom lost their own lives trying to save others.

THE FORECAST CALLED FOR "RAIN TONIGHT," WHICH DID not seem unusual, as it had been raining for three days straight, and the ground was sodden from an unusually wet summer and fall. What was a little more rain?

Weston Historical Society

Weston Historical Society

For days, buried in the back pages, the newspapers had been describing the destruction caused in Haiti and the Dominican Republic by a hurricane called Hazel. It was a busy year for hurricanes, with seven female-monikered monsters having already crawled up the East Coast. This one seemed no different. For Torontonians, hurricanes were nothing to fear. They rarely reached southern Ontario. Hurricanes often take a direct

Eric E.H. Taylor/Toronto Port Authority/PC 11 125

Eric E.H. Taylor/Toronto Port Authority/PC 11 128

route north from the Caribbean to the Golden Horseshoe, but long before they ever reach Ontario they curl away back out into the Atlantic Ocean. Hurricanes often lash the Carolinas, smashing houses and boats and submerging coastal towns from Myrtle Beach north to Wilmington. The great storms push inland north towards Pennsylvania, losing steam as they encounter the Allegheny Mountains and are pushed offshore, scattering fishing boats and other vessels before they peter out over empty waters.

Hurricanes are the most awesome force on the planet. Swirling masses of wind and rain, they can grow to more than one hundred miles wide. Their winds can reach 175

Sunnyside Beach resembled a clear-cut after Hazel unexpectedly moved north across New York and cut a swath directly through Toronto. Debris surged onto the beaches, covering them with driftwood, refuse, and remnants of lives from the northeastern United States and Ontario.

miles per hour, with gusts up to 200 miles per hour. Over the centuries they have killed hundreds of thousands of unsuspecting people, many in their own homes.

Hurricanes are formed in the warm, moist air that lies over the ocean. At first they exist as small disturbances, their winds slight, with a barometer reading just lower than normal. But they grow quickly. In only a few days the winds jump to 50 and then up to 150 miles per hour. Fuelled by the tropical waters, the storms move northward, where the water becomes cooler and they often deteriorate and fade away. But sometimes a storm finds a way to push farther west and north, where it chooses its path: the Caribbean, the Gulf of Mexico, or the Carolinas.

Hurricanes kill in many ways. The wind picks up and throws whatever is in its path, ripping up stop signs and fence posts and hurling them around suburbs like spears. Roofing tiles whiz

Above left: Few possessions remained when the Humber River poured through doors and windows of homes in Weston.

Left: This woman seems remarkably upbeat as she trucks some of her belongings around in a hamper.

through gale-force winds like giant blades. The winds knock over houses and marinas. Sudden surges shove cars off roads and into ditches or other cars, the drivers blinded completely when the wipers are torn away. Many drive straight into rivers, unaware that the approach has been washed away.

Hurricanes mostly drown. The volume of water that pours down during a hurricane is beyond belief. It rains so hard that while you are taking the time to marvel at just how much, the water rises around you. Within only a couple of hours the water can rise past your knees. It squeezes under the front door of your house, then knocks the door down and gushes up the stairwell. Rivers swell beyond their banks, turning streets into streams, backyards and

Weston Historical Society

Boatloads of volunteers scan the river for bodies.

town squares into lakes. Everything in the path of the rushing water becomes a deadly weapon. The detritus of everyday life gnashes and spins in a lethal, swirling tangle that knocks down houses and drowns and crushes those who have failed to escape to higher ground.

Hurricanes are given people's names — Camille, Andrew, Floyd, Carol. Originally only women's names were used. At the end of the nineteenth century, Clement Wragge, a meteorologist for the government of Queensland, Australia, named hurricanes after women and local political figures he particularly disliked so that Australians could put a face to the howling, insane creatures that threatened the shipping lanes. Some speculate that it became the practice to name the storms after women after the publication of

Weston Historical Society

the novel *Storm* by George R. Stewart, in which the protagonist bestows women's names upon hurricanes without the knowledge of his superiors. At various times the American military has given the storms women's names, has used the phonetic system "Able, Baker, Charlie," or has labelled them with the storm's latitude and longitude. Today, every other storm bears a man's name.

We remember the worst storms, but quickly forget the tempests that hover offshore on satellite weather maps only to dissipate long before they make landfall. We remember Hurricane Andrew, of course, which

Martin Taylor

Weston Historical Society

demolished Florida in 1992. We remember Hurricane Floyd, which careered into North Carolina in 1999. Thanks to Erik Larson's book *Isaac's Storm*, we read, fascinated, about the nameless storm that turned Galveston, Texas, into a modern Atlantis in 1900, killing approximately eight thousand people.

Florida, the Carolinas, Texas — prime targets for Atlantic storms. But Ontario? The chances of the province seeing the serious effects of a hurricane have been calculated at 1 percent in any given year. A few storms have threatened to follow Hazel's path to Toronto, most recently Isabel in 2003, which batted around a few lawn chairs and garbage tins and disappointed thousands who looked forward to the novelty of a northern hurricane. The newspapers hailed Isabel as the return of Hurricane Hazel. Reporters combed coffee shops and malls for those who remembered the night of October 15, 1954.

The 48th Highlanders, trucked in to assist in search operations, take a well-deserved lunch break.

Gordon W. Powley/Archives of Ontario/C 5-2-2-33-1/10002916

Most remember Hazel as a bad rainstorm. They went to bed and woke up to a changed city. Some spent the night pumping out their basements or driving towards higher ground to weather the storm in front of a roaring fire far from the flood water. For hundreds of others, however, it was a horrific night: houses being torn from their foundations to become sinking boats, neighbours floating by clinging to what was left of their roofs. When the call rang out for volunteers, many left the relative safety of their homes and families and ventured out into that dark, terrible night.

Born in early October off the west coast of Africa, Hazel drew its power from the heated waters of the Atlantic and blazed towards the Caribbean. On October 5, the storm roared fifty miles off the coast of Grenada, and on October 6 it passed between the islands of Grenada and Carriacou. From there Hazel sidled west at 15 miles per hour, with the barometer reading a low of 29.44 inches and winds reaching 110 miles per hour. On October 7, the pressure dropped to 29.12 inches and winds whipped up to 125 miles per hour as Hazel neared Haiti, curling around the western tip of the island nation but not sparing its inhabitants her wrath. Nearly one thousand people were killed as houses were flattened and landslides buried island residents. On October 13, Hazel began to turn north, with winds reaching 100 miles per hour, and the great storm increased its speed as it raced towards the Atlantic seaboard.

Early on October 15, North and South Carolina residents were warned that Hazel was on the way. At 9:25 A.M., when most Torontonians were just settling in at work or beginning their daily chores, Hazel battered Myrtle Beach, the barometer dropping to 28.47 inches. Over the next few hours the barometer dropped steadily, Hazel's

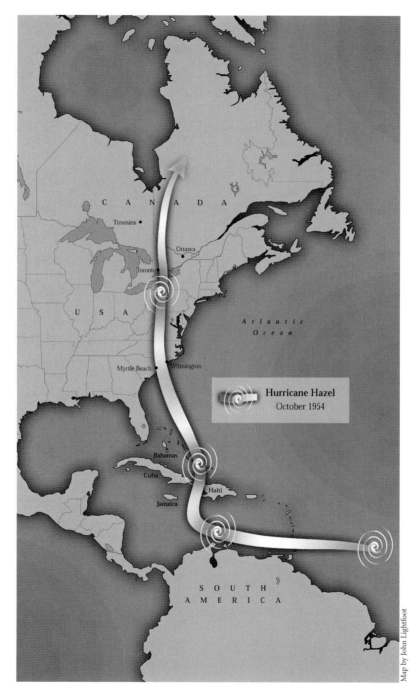

Map by John Lightfoot

HURRICANE HAZEL
Canada's Storm of the Century

Weston Historical Society

Weston Historical Society

winds screamed at 125 miles per hour, and the storm moved at 60 miles per hour north overland. At one point, Hazel was 120 miles wide, and her gales reached a width of 200 miles.

Typically, hurricanes lose steam and dissipate after having made landfall, but Hazel was no ordinary storm. Fed by a cold front that had moved east across the Rockies, which on its own could have produced a severe storm, Hazel picked up speed and moved north through North Carolina, Virginia, West Virginia, and Washington, D.C., setting records for rainfall and high winds, which ranged between 130 and 150 miles per hour, taking many lives and wreaking unfathomable damage. At Long Beach along the coast of North Carolina, Hazel left behind only 5 of the 357 buildings along the shore. After the storm, survivors found palm fronds and wooden bowls inscribed "Made in Haiti" along the Carolina coast.

"It took the whole side of my house out," said Dick Ford, who was building a new home in Maryland. Hazel tore off the roof and chimney of his neighbour's house and flung it three hundred feet into his. Ellen Ford remembers the wind picking up her father's skipjack and dropping it in their front yard. "The anchor cut a trench in the road."

As Torontonians were preparing to pack it up for the weekend, Hazel pushed over the Allegheny Mountains and through New York State towards Lake Ontario. At 6:00 P.M., with the eye of the storm nearing Lake Ontario, the winds lessened to 70 miles per hour. In Syracuse, New York, Hazel tore down the marquee of the Elmwood Theater. It had read, "Now Playing: *Gone with the Wind*."

There is much dispute about whether the residents of Toronto and the surrounding areas were forewarned about the hurricane. Many people do not remember having heard an announcement on the radio, and certainly not on their televisions.

On Friday morning, Fred Turnbull of the Malton Dominion Public Weather Office watched Hazel closely. The office released a forecast at 9:30 A.M. calling for continuous rain throughout the day. Turnbull believed that the rainfall over the next twenty-four hours could exceed the heaviest on record. The office released a second statement:

> The present Northerly motion of the hurricane centre is causing considerable apprehension in Southern Ontario areas … the Allegheny mountain range lies between us and the storm centre. The mountain range may break up, or materially weaken, the storm's intensity, or cause it to veer off towards the Northeast. Just what effect the Allegheny mountains will have cannot be stated at the moment, but a further bulletin will be issued by noon today.

Weston Historical Society

Houses resemble flattened packing crates in Weston, shot through with telephone poles and tree trunks.

That noon forecast suggested that "in crossing the Allegheny mountains the hurricane will decrease markedly in intensity with winds not expected to exceed 50 miles per hour on the open water of Lake Ontario."

At 9:30 P.M., as many huddled with the wind and rain howling at their windows, this forecast was issued: "The intensity of this storm has decreased to the point where it should no longer be classified as a hurricane. This weakening storm will continue northward, passing just east of Toronto before midnight. The main rainfall associated with it should end shortly thereafter, with occasional light rain occurring throughout the night."

Though Turnbull, the officer in charge of the weather office, had predicted possible record rainfalls with analysis from his colleague Norman Grundy, and despite two warnings that Hazel had made it over the Alleghenies, the official reports did not alarm the residents of Toronto. Many assumed that the city was in for a rocky, though safe, night.

A S COMMUTERS CRAWLED UP THE CITY'S ARTERIES TOWARDS their homes on the outskirts or rode the streetcar or subway in anticipation of a quiet night in front of the television, people started to notice that this was not just a bad rainstorm.

At its worst, Hurricane Hazel was a category four storm on the Saffir-Simpson scale, which ranks it in select company with the past century's most vicious storms. But as Hazel's eye moved over Lake Ontario, the storm was downgraded from a hurricane to an extratropical cyclone. The winds eased as Hazel mixed with the much colder storm heading east. Technically, the hurricane that has lived in the memories of Canadians from Niagara Falls to Uxbridge to Timmins was no longer a hurricane when it crossed the border. But no one remembers the storm that hit southern Ontario in October 1954 as Extratropical Cyclone Hazel.

Weston Historical Society

"At six o'clock the sky was black and there was two inches of water on the ground," remembers Nick Chometa, then a fourteen-year-old boy living in Toronto's west end. "I couldn't see more than a few feet in front of me, couldn't see the sides of the road. I drove down a ditch into a culvert and bent in the bumper of my dad's new car, then backed up and went home. My father wasn't too angry about my getting into an accident in his car because you just could not see in the storm," he recalls.

"I sat at my desk and looked out the window at the rain coming down. It was almost five and we could go home. I left the office at Bay and Front and took a streetcar home. Leaving the centre doors from the streetcar, I stepped down into what I thought was a big puddle. I made my way to the curb, but where was it?" recalls Joyce Walker. "I remember a man took my hand and led

Archives of Ontario/RG 14 B-10-2 #422, 6

me to the sidewalk. The water was so deep that it went right over the curb. That night we listened to the news on the radio. Little did we know of the tragic events that were to follow that night. A big puddle on Bloor Street seems so small compared to the loss of so many."

Mary Jane Thorne-Rees, who was on her way home from a piano lesson near Avenue Road and Davenport, will never forget the storm. "The neighbours across the road were hosting a bridal shower. I was a drowned rat by the time I got home. I couldn't join my mom and grandmother as they went to the shower. We sure got much more than a shower that night."

Sheets of rain blinded drivers as they approached damaged bridges and washouts. Cars were washed downstream or, like this one, hit an earth wall and were crushed.

27

The Queensbury Hotel, a notorious watering hole on Scarlett Road, withstood Hazel's fury.

Al Brierley was on his way home from his shift at Mack Trucks. "I drove through the rain up to where we lived in the Dufferin and Glencairn area," he recalls. "I had trouble getting through the underpass at King and Dufferin because of all of the water." The next morning, Brierley found that the tires were flat on one side of his car. Pushing through the rain and debris, he had driven through the storm without realizing he had two blowouts.

North of the city, from Markham to Woodbridge to Holland Landing up to Barrie, the rains and winds from Hazel pounded unsuspecting people going about their daily lives. Frank Orr, who would later become a Hockey Hall of Fame sports reporter with the *Toronto Star*, was living on a farm near the village of Hillsburgh and attending Guelph Collegiate. "I went to a high school football game that Friday afternoon and doubt if I ever have been as wet as I was from the opening deluge

Millions of gallons of water invaded homes and businesses all around the city. Only the roof and radio antenna of this car, submerged in a garage, remain visible.

Farms all over southern Ontario were inundated by flood water. This barn near Cookstown became an island sanctuary for livestock.

29

of rain." For more than an hour during the ride home in a school bus along the country roads, Orr worried that the wind would push the bus off the road. He arrived home to find the farm under assault from the wind and rain. "Our farm buildings were at the end of a long lane with a considerable slope and that evening the equivalent of the Mississippi came down the lane and through our stable, where we milked thirty Jersey cows, their feet covered in water," he recalls. "The only word to describe that night, even fifty miles from Toronto, is hairy. All the gravel on the lane, including stones of a size not usually moved in that situation, was in the barnyard."

John Thurston knew the rain was coming, but after his day at British American Oil in downtown Toronto, he ventured home to prepare for a double date at Casa Loma. "I took the subway north to Eglinton and then found that there was a big puddle in the intersection of Yonge and Lawrence. Then I went and picked up my date and we went to Casa Loma, where there was a live orchestra and a dance. I drove around in the rainstorm to get there, and drove home in the pounding rain." Thurston went to bed, unaware of the drama unfolding throughout the city.

Ken Gibbs was delivering furniture for Eaton's in the west end during the day of the storm. "My delivery route took me back and forth on

Downtown Toronto resembled Venice on the night of October 15, 1954. Streetlights glimmered over the flooded intersection of King and John.

Bloor and Dundas streets and over such rivers and creeks as the Humber, Mimico, and Etobicoke," he recalls. "At one particular home I carried a large mattress to be delivered and thought I would be lifted off the ground by the terrific force of the now mounting wind. At the next home — it was in the Kingsway area of Toronto — the delivery could not be made because the driveway of the home at the sidewalk was completely washed away."

Having finished his deliveries as best he could, Gibbs decided to head home, but he found himself stranded on the west side of the Humber. "At the old town of Islington I decided to telephone home to say I would be late. As I made the call I saw the creek at Islington Avenue and Dundas Street overflow into a used car lot and lift the automobiles like little blocks of wood and send them crashing into each other."

Above left: *Thousands of gallons of water crushed the bungalows as if they were nothing more than dollhouses.*

Above right: *Hazel sheared off one end of this house, heaving it off its foundations and against another building.*

31

This house was flooded as high as the light fixtures.

When the flood water receded, only damaged furniture, odds and ends, and a few inches of silt on the floor remained.

At 11:00 P.M. on October 15, 1954, Hazel officially hit Toronto, but in the hours before, as the eye had neared the city, the fury of the storm had already caused unbelievable damage. Roads and underpasses were flooded. Water poured in through basement windows, especially in the west end. Bridge abutments over the Humber and Don rivers and Etobicoke and Mimico creeks wore down under the constant pounding of the cresting flood water. Motorists became stranded when roads washed out in front of them. The roads jammed when cars were abandoned as the water inched its way up to the door handles. Some made it to safety before the situation became too treacherous, but others had nowhere to go and climbed onto their cars or into trees to escape the torrent.

Toronto Police Museum

Raymore Drive. Most of the houses in this photo were torn down; the land was appropriated by the city's conservation authority and turned into parkland.

The city's west end bore the brunt of the storm. The Humber River, which snakes south from Woodbridge through Etobicoke and into Lake Ontario, became a lethal, writhing mass of water and debris. The Humber poured over its banks and tore through houses and cottages all along its route. In Long Branch, in the southwest of the city, Hazel took seven lives in a cottage settlement and the Pleasant Valley Trailer Park. The river uprooted trees, houses, and garages and sent them tumbling southward in the roiling river, joining all kinds of items stolen from people's lives: bicycles, dolls, cars, hockey sticks, fence posts, timbers from barns, shoes.

33

Though it has sustained some damage, this bungalow stands like an oasis among what remains of the houses around it. The water line from the flood runs just under the window ledges.

Toronto Police Museum

Toronto and Region Conservation Authority

In Woodbridge, to the northwest of Toronto, residents of a trailer park were sleeping through the storm when an earthen dam collapsed, sending millions of tons of water into the camp, twirling and crushing the trailers like tin cans. At least twenty residents were killed, and many were left homeless. The water unleashed from the Woodbridge dam funnelled south along the Humber, which became a violent juggernaut that surged over its banks into unsuspecting villages along its shoreline.

In nearby Kleinburg, the George family, who lived in a Macedonian enclave on Broda Drive, barely escaped the flood. "I was two at the time and

This helicopter might be flying over a battlefield, not a quiet Toronto neighbourhood.

34

was staying with my grandmother," remembers Edith George. "Everybody was crying. That night, my mother was running up and down the streets trying to find me and my family. Dad had been at a poker game. We all escaped the flooding in my granddad's new Buick."

Today the Humber River Valley in Etobicoke is a city park, lined by ribbons of bicycle and pedestrian paths. In 1954, people still lived along the banks of the Humber in the floodplain. The residents of Weston, Swansea, and Long Branch were used to flooding, but had always seen it as an annual nuisance rather than as a threat.

Stan Elphick's father just made it onto one of the last buses home to Weston before the flooding blocked the roads. "About 11:30 P.M. he called us to tell about his harrowing experience. He had managed to get to the bus stop for the Weston bus at Weston Road and St. Clair. He had waited in a coffee shop to get out of the pouring rain. After ten to fifteen minutes, a bus driver announced he was going to make a trip

Pitched on their sides and full of muck, the trailers at the Woodbridge camp were no longer inhabitable. Survivors of the carnage lived in temporary housing on the Woodbridge Fairgrounds, awaiting construction of a new development.

35

This house on Raymore Drive in Weston, twisted and wrenched off its foundations, resembles an accordion.

Toronto Police Museum

to Weston but this was going to be the last run for the evening," recalls Elphick. "He told the passengers that there was considerable flooding at Weston Road where Black Creek flows under the road. Weston Road was flooded but the driver said he would try to get through. At the lowest point, the water completely covered the wheels but fortunately the bus kept going and Dad finally arrived home, soaking wet."

Raymore Drive was just another street in Weston near Lawrence Avenue

Ted Grant/National Archives of Canada/E002107655

Courtesy of John Elphick

Above: *Hazel took so much from so many, and ruined what was left behind. Residents hung clothesline upon clothesline of sheets and undergarments in the crisp early winter wind.*

Left: *John Elphick captured the destruction revealed by the daylight on the Saturday after the storm in this vivid painting.*

Lake Simcoe

Barrie

Beeton

Bradford
Holland Marsh

Aurora

Uxbridge

Bolton

Kleinburg

Woodbridge

Thornhill

Humber River

Holland River

Don River

Brampton

Long Branch

Toronto

Lake Ontario

Humber River - Weston

McDonald-Cartier Freeway (401)

Fair Glen Cres.

Dixon Rd.

Lawrence Ave.

WESTON

Raymore Dr.
Kingdom St.
Tilden Cres.

Weston Rd.

Eglinton Ave.

Royal York Rd.

Scarlett Rd.

Black Creek

Dundas St.

Jane St.

Humber River

Park Lawn Cemetery

Bloor St.

Gardiner Expwy.

Lake Ontario

Map by John Lightfoot

38

and Scarlett Road, right along the banks of the Humber. Many generations shared the houses along Raymore, saving up for the day when some of them could move out on their own. It was a nice neighbourhood, low-key, unremarkable, but comfortable.

As the Humber swelled only a few yards away, longtime locals watched warily, but were not overly concerned. Around the dinner

The dotted line that runs horizontally demonstrates where a swing bridge once stood. When the bridge broke away, it moved several feet, but its steel cables held firm and it directed the gushing flood right at Raymore Drive.

The newspapers would refer to Raymore Drive, which ran right along the Humber River, as the "Street That Never Was."

Weston Historical Society

This water filtration plant near Raymore Drive was besieged by the Humber.

hour, some residents walked up and down Raymore Drive and neighbouring streets suggesting that people seek the safety of higher ground, perhaps at the Army-Navy Club on Kingdom Street. One longtime resident convinced some to stay in their homes despite the warnings, a decision that cost many their lives.

Dave Iris, who lived on Brownlea Avenue in Westmount, near Raymore Drive, was six years old at the time. "I remember coming home from Humber Heights School that day, in the rain. That night my dad opened a little window in our house, looked out, and said, 'There are people who are going to drown out there tonight.' I said, 'Are we going to drown?' He told me that we weren't," Iris says. "I lost neighbours and school chums on Raymore Drive. We had a few inches of water in the basement, but only a few houses away, people died."

Later in the evening, over the river near Raymore Drive, a swing bridge began to buckle and bend under the weight of the water. As nearby residents waited out the storm in their bungalows, one end of the bridge broke free of its abutment and began to swing out over the river. The suspension wires held the bridge after it had moved a few feet, but the bridge now blocked the river, redirecting the water and debris over the banks of the Humber and right at Raymore Drive. One minute the water roared past the backyards of the quiet street, the next it smashed into the houses.

Dave Phillips, on his way home from a date with his fiancée, was witness to the destruction. "The homes were literally lifted off their foundations and swept away. You could hear the people screaming. Many of them were standing on their roofs. In many cases the screaming just stopped; the homes just disintegrated, and that was the end of it."

Raymore residents Annie and Joe Ward woke up at midnight, water already in their house and rising. They took their wire-haired terrier, Lassie, and crawled up into the attic. With the house beginning to collapse around them, they climbed up into the rafters. Joe dug at the roof with screwdriver and fingernails, ripping a hole just big enough for them to fit through. Lassie was left behind, wrapped in a blanket. On the roof, the beam of a flashlight showed that their house was up

Toronto Telegram/York University Archives 1752

Firefighters escort a frightened Weston resident out of the swirling river. Many went to bed and woke up to flooded basements, while one street over firefighters, police officers, and volunteers mined the river for survivors until daylight.

Raymore Drive was almost completely wiped out during Hazel.

against another house, and the tangled mass of wood and windows was floating down the river. The Wards jumped from their roof onto the roof of their neighbours, the Andersons, and watched from comparative safety. As the wind and rain wailed around the Wards in their inadequate clothing, they saw flashlight beams moving up the stairwells in other houses as their neighbours tried to escape, but the houses would tear away from their foundations and the flashlights would go out. The Wards survived the night, as did Lassie, who had somehow escaped the mayhem.

The house that once stood at 148 Raymore Drive suffered the most

This aerial shot of Raymore Drive demonstrates the seeming randomness of a hurricane's wrath. Some houses still stood after the street was bombarded by a wall of water, while others were reduced to their cinder-block foundations.

tragic loss, with the Edwards and Neil families, who shared the dwelling, losing nine family members. Mr. and Mrs. Charles Edwards lost six grandchildren, their son and daughter-in-law, and their daughter. John Neil, another resident of 148 Raymore and husband of the Edwardses' daughter, arrived home at 1:30 A.M. to find his street washed away, and, thinking that his family had been evacuated, he joined the ongoing volunteer efforts. Not until 10:00 A.M. on Saturday would the Edwardses and John Neil receive word that their family was gone. Neil searched the riverbanks of the Humber for days afterwards with his dog in a fruitless search for the bodies of his lost kin. Hurricane Hazel killed thirty-two people on Raymore Drive, and left sixty families homeless. A section of the street more than twelve hundred feet long was erased, only upturned earth and rubble remaining where people had once lived.

Norma Vineham was working at her corner store at Lawrence Avenue and Weston Road the night of Hurricane Hazel. "The firemen kept coming into the store to get pop. At one point they said that they wouldn't be coming back again because they would be rescuing people, and we closed the store," she says. "The next day, when the piano tuner came for an appointment, my daughters, who went to school with some of the kids from Raymore Drive, asked him if those children were okay, but he didn't know."

Wallace Rombough of the Weston Police Department went to bed thinking the storm had about blown itself out, but was awakened at 2:00 A.M. by Lew Everist, also of the Weston police, who told him that "the Humber River had overflowed its banks, the houses were being washed away and people drowning." At Downsview, with Squadron Leader Malcolm Cliff of the RCAF Reserve, Rombough searched the banks of the Humber in a sixteen-foot boat. Under the lights of a CBC television crew, Cliff and Rombough inched upstream, where they found a couple stranded in trees. "As we approached," remembers Rombough, "the woman panicked and jumped into the

Weston Historical Society

The St. Phillips Road bridge in Weston was fully immersed at the height of the storm.

water just before we reached her. She went under but popped up like a cork and I was able to grab her by the hair and pull her into the boat." The man kept his calm and climbed into the boat. After rescuing two young men from an upturned boat, and with their own boat in disrepair, the weary rescuers retired to the Martindale Lodge on Albion Road for sandwiches and rye and ginger ale.

At Fair Glen Crescent, off St. Phillips Road south of Albion Road, two complete strangers risked their own lives to save dozens of the area's unsuspecting residents.

Weston Historical Society

Jim Crawford was a twenty-four-year-old off-duty police constable with the North York police. He was new to the force, having spent some time in James Bay working for the Hudson Bay Company in the fur department. At 6′ 4″ and 240 pounds, Crawford was an imposing figure. He felt it was his duty to go to the river to see what he could do. He said to his brother Patrick, "Let's go over to the Humber. We can make heroes of ourselves tonight."

Herb Jones, a local contractor, had brought his boat down to the foot of Fair Glen, on the river, when he heard that people were in trouble.

Left: *These two boys found refuge atop a car, their clothing soaked, their feet and legs bare on a cold October night. Like many young people, these boys appear to have found Hurricane Hazel to be a grand adventure.*

Below left and right and opposite (top): *North York Police Constable Jim Crawford and contractor Herb Jones paired up in a small boat with a testy motor to search the Humber River, starting out at the foot of Fair Glen Crescent, shown here. Houses from Fair Glen down to Raymore Drive were set afloat when the river wrested them from their foundations. Crawford and Jones pulled helpless families off roofs and out of trees. They wouldn't see each other again for more than thirty years.*

Toronto Telegram/York University Archives 1334

City of Toronto Archives, series 6, item 63

City of Toronto Archives, series 6, item 62

The Crawford brothers drove from Downsview down to the turbulent river, water already up to the hood of the car. "I was completely flabbergasted by the height that the water had risen to," Jim Crawford would later recall. "The river was just unbelievably swollen. Many people were trapped on roofs and porches." Herb Jones, his boat ready to go out, asked for volunteers. "I'll go with you," said Crawford. He hopped in the boat and waved a handheld spotlight at the houses and trees as Jones navigated the precarious waters. At first they rescued people off the porches of their homes, then off the upstairs porches, then off the roofs.

"We didn't have time to play around with how we were getting them off the roof and into the boat. If we didn't get them off we were on our way to Lake Ontario ourselves," says Crawford. As the two novice rescuers approached one man stranded on the roof of his house, he waved them away towards other houses with families atop them. "He didn't make it," remembers Crawford. After they dropped off more passengers, Herb Jones

Martin Taylor

Firefighters from across Toronto, on call or not, rushed to the Humber when the call went out that people were drowning. These rescuers organized under intense searchlights, others worked by the lights of CBC television cameras, but many rescuers waded through the darkness guided only by hand-held flashlights and the feeble cries of Hazel's victims.

Toronto and Region Conservation Authority

47

HURRICANE HAZEL
Canada's Storm of the Century

Many west-end residents discovered too late that the flood water had surrounded their houses. Many, like the Robinson family, took what they could and climbed up ladders, trees, even chesterfields to reach the comparative safety of the roofs of their houses. Several families awoke to find their living room furniture floating around the main floor, and, too late to make it out the door, they clawed holes in the roofs with screwdrivers and hatchets and awaited rescue atop their homes.

asked Crawford if he was ready for another go at the river. Crawford recalls, "I said to him, 'I'm game if you're game.'"

At one house, Tom Doucette was trapped with his wife and kids and an elderly lady, a neighbour they had taken in when they saw that the river was rising. "We were taking them off the roof and the house next door started to break free and crashed into the Doucette house. We got the wife and two kids and said we'd be back for him and the lady," Crawford recalls. "The lady was swept off the roof and was trapped in the trees. Doucette took a hatchet and chopped a hole through the roof to pull the old lady back onto the house. Herb nosed into the trees and grabbed the lady by the fanny of her clothing, and then we rescued Doucette."

At one point a shear pin broke in the motor, and the two were stranded on the raging river. Jones, an expert boatman, held onto a tree with one hand and repaired the motor with the other while Crawford held the spotlight.

Only after they had rescued as many people as they possibly could did they head back to shore. "We went out until there were no houses or garages left. I don't know how many trips we made, but we saved fifty or sixty people. I still get cards of thanks from some of the families."

After the final trip Jones and Crawford went their separate ways. Soon after the night of Hurricane Hazel, Crawford was promoted to detective. Later he became a prominent homicide detective with the Toronto police force, until he retired in 1988. Crawford lost touch with Herb Jones, a stranger with whom he had shared a treacherous few hours dusting the waves of the swollen Humber River in a small boat.

"About a year after I retired," recalls Crawford, "I heard that Herb was sick. I had kept in touch with the Jones family, but I hadn't seen Herb since that day. I went to Sunnybrook Hospital and reintroduced myself. He appreciated the visit. We talked a lot on the phone after that. He died a few months later."

The day after the storm, survivors and curiosity seekers walked down Fair Glen Crescent, where nearly twenty homes were demolished. "Grotesque, lopsided houses sagged or lay in every imaginable position," reported the *Globe and Mail*. "Tops and hoods of cars protruded above the water, marking the place where Fair Glen Crescent bends and follows the river-front." Some of the houses of Fair Glen had been carried downstream and smashed against the concrete pillars of a railway trestle near the Lakeshore.

Along the nearby Etobicoke Creek, sixteen-year-old beauty school student Sylvia Jones (now Sylvia Cutajar) and her family had just returned home when it became

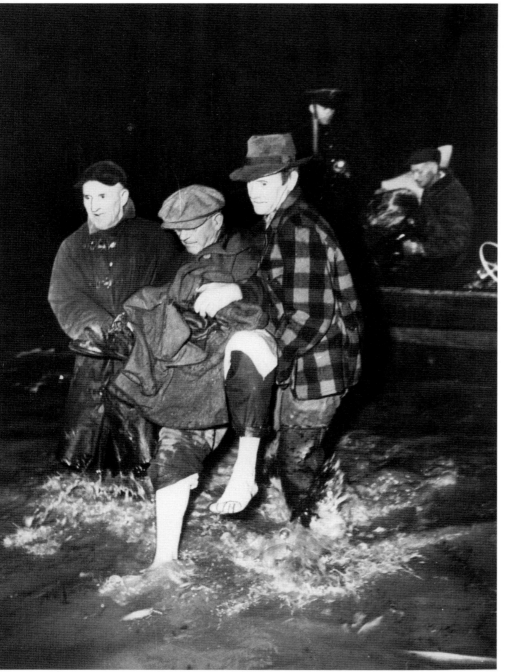

Toronto Telegram/York University Archives 219

apparent that the storm was raging out of control. But they weren't worried — at least not until the water rose a few feet in only an hour. Soon the Joneses were climbing a ladder at the back of their house up to the roof. From their own roof the Joneses watched as across the street another family, the Thorpes, found themselves in the same predicament. A local volunteer fire department strung ropes along the hydro wires from one side of the street to the other and pulled themselves along in a boat, intent on rescuing the Thorpes.

On the first trip along the rescue line, the firemen returned with nine-month-old Nancy Thorpe and handed her to Sylvia. The rescuers then slowly pulled themselves back across to the Thorpe house, only to find that the rest of the Thorpe family had been washed

One of the lucky. Jim Crawford, Herb Jones, Wallace Rombough, and other volunteers plied the raging Humber in small boats and saved everyone they could.

away. Huddled on the rooftop of her family home, Sylvia held onto baby Nancy for the rest of the night until she could finally hand her to Red Cross workers, who took her to nearby St. Joseph's Hospital. In the days after the storm, Nancy would appear, crying and rankled, on the front pages of newspapers across the country, and for many she would become a symbol of the lost. Nancy's grandparents adopted the little girl and changed her name. Today, no one except her family knows what has become of her.

Everyone who remembers the night of Hazel remembers the tragic loss of the five firefighters of the Kingsway-Lambton Fire Department.

At 1:09 A.M. on October 16, Deputy Fire Chief Clarence "Tiny" Collins, along with firefighters Jim Britton, Roy Oliver, Jack Phillips, Dave Palmateer, Marsh Palmateer, and Angus Small, was dispatched to River Road on the Humber, where people were reportedly stranded on a car.

The firemen, raced to the scene in a pumper; Frank Mercer, from the same firehouse, followed behind in his car. A mile south of Dundas Street, near Bloor, the crew found the road awash and decided to back the truck up the street. Mercer's car stalled, and the pumper, with Oliver at the wheel, tried to push it out of their way. The truck became stuck in the water and mud, so the firemen decided to wait out the storm on their vehicle. Mercer's car began to float away in the current, so the others threw him a rope and he joined them on the pumper. With the truck's lights blazing, the firemen called for rescue on their police radio.

As Fire Chief Bill Bell called out from the riverbank, other firemen and rescuers readied themselves to save their comrades. Britton tied a rope around himself and walked towards a chain-link fence on shore. The water pushed him back to the truck.

The firefighters climbed onto the ladder as the water swirled ever higher around them. The flood whisked away a thousand-foot firehose in seconds. Police officers from Etobicoke tried to launch a boat, but the current would not allow it. The truck began to float downstream. As it threatened to capsize, the men shook hands, said "good luck," and jumped into the wash.

Jim Britton was snagged by a tree. Nearby, Frank Mercer called weakly for help. A human chain could not reach him in time, and he was swept away. Police rescued Britton and Jack Phillips. Marsh Palmateer managed to swim to shore. Frank Mercer and the remaining four — Clarence Collins, Roy Oliver, Dave Palmateer, and Angus Small — were lost. The next day the truck was found several hundred feet south near the parking lot of the Old Mill Restaurant, crushed, the ladder ripped away.

Toronto and Region Conservation Authority

Firefighters and interested locals descend upon the crushed remains of the Kingsway-Lambton fire truck lost during the night. The five volunteers who manned this truck, responding to a report of stranded motorists, were lost when flood water first encircled then swallowed the truck. Clarence "Tiny" Collins, Frank Mercer, Roy Oliver, Dave Palmateer, and Angus Small have long been celebrated as heroes of the storm.

As the tragedy of the Kingsway-Lambton fire crew unfolded, other rescue operations continued.

Telephone linesman Gerald Elliot was driving across the Old Mill Bridge when it collapsed, sending him into the water. Firefighters threw him a hose and began to pull him towards shore. The hose snapped. Elliot became caught in the current, but soon grabbed onto a willow tree, where he was stranded. Max Hurley,

J.V. Salmon/Toronto Public Library T33233

This Kingsway-Lambton fire truck replaced the one lost during Hurricane Hazel.

of the Harbour Police, borrowed Dr. Bernard Willinsky's new black Cadillac, which Jack "Hot-shot" Russell had parked in the Harbour Police garage for safekeeping. Hurley strapped a dinghy to the roof of the car. When Russell asked what Hurley was doing, he replied, "I've commandeered your Caddy for an adventure. Hop in, Hot-shot!" Hurley tied a rope around his waist and pulled himself along the edge of the river towards Elliot, without success. Repeated rescue attempts by rope, ladder, and helicopter failed. Finally, with Elliot's lips blue and his strength waning, Hurley steered the dinghy close to him, and he jumped into the stern. After reaching shore, Elliot was rushed to St. Joseph's Hospital, where he was treated for exposure and shock.

Crews of the fledgling CBC television news captured some of the terror of that night as they lit up the river for rescuers. Surviving footage shows residents scampering to safety in heavy rain. Dark, foreboding music dubbed over the footage provides eerie, yet suitable, accompaniment to the scenes of devastation.

HURRICANE HAZEL
Canada's Storm of the Century

On October 16, the day after the storm, the Old Mill Bridge still lies nearly submerged in the Humber. The approach on the east side of the bridge was washed away late the day before. Unsuspecting motorists, including Gerald Elliot, drove headlong into the river without ever realizing that the bridge was out.

"It was a wind with a woman's name that caused the trouble … Hazel, fickle and frantic, had come to call with all her fury," says the sombre narrator. As Holst's "Mars" from *The Planets* suite rages in the background, CBC reporter Ian MacIntosh asks a man whose family is marooned on a rooftop if he is worried. "I'd like to get them out of there as soon as I could," the man responds.

At the end of Humberview Crescent, across from the Weston Golf and Country Club, Weston resident Marj Mossman watched the Humber rising from high above the river. "I walked out with my dad to see what was going on, but it was too dangerous, and I went back in. I remember sparks as houses came unleashed from hydro wires."

Mossman was amazed at the dramatic change that Hazel caused in the Humber. "We could always hear the river from our house, a steady hum, but that night it roared. It must have been awfully frightening for the people living on lower ground."

In Long Branch, along the shores of Lake Ontario, Mildred Denby and Bessie Young of the Red Cross heard faint cries from an abandoned house at about 1:00 A.M. They found an elderly woman, Helen Puddister, lying in a few inches of water. A policeman helped tear the door off the house, and they used it as a stretcher to carry the woman for a mile through muck and brush to a Red Cross truck. After delivering Mrs. Puddister to the truck, Denby and Young returned to their rescue efforts.

Nelson and Winnie McLean, along with their two children, four-month-old Sue and fourteen-month-old Calvin, lived along Black Creek in a two-bedroom house in Islington. While they were watching television, the screen suddenly went blank. Winnie went outside to see if the aerial had blown off the roof. "When I stepped out the door, there was a calmness, a stillness in the air much like after a storm," she recalls. "As we couldn't watch out favourite programs on TV, and since the storm appeared to be over, we retired for the night, unaware of the terrible events that were soon to unfold." At 1:00 A.M. they heard someone knocking at their window pleading with them to get out. "We went out to take a look at what was going on and were surprised to see water in the front and back yard running fast and deep." They grabbed what they could, bundled their babies in blankets, and walked out into waist-deep water. Firemen carried their children to safety and tied ropes around the McLeans, showing them to another rope that had been strung up the embankment to higher ground. From there, a chilling sight. "We could see the two-storey Scarlett Road Hotel, with the flood water running through the upper windows and out the back," McLean recalls. "The most pathetic and heart-rending sight we saw were cars floating by with people clinging desperately on top crying for help. Other people were halfway up hydro poles waiting to be rescued, but before long the surging waters claimed them."

The Humber was not the only river raging out of control. Across the city, the Don River, which cuts south through the eastern half of Toronto, overflowed its banks as well. Had the storm hovered over the Don as it had over the Humber, the river would likely have decimated the housing along its banks. Nevertheless, it was still a dangerous night for several people unfortunate enough to be caught out in the storm of the century.

Alex Nicholson, a salesman who lived on Pottery Road near a bridge over the Don, was trapped for five and a half hours in the swirling morass. Aware that the river was flooding around the dam, Nicholson had been stopping cars from trying to cross the bridge. As he went to get a change of clothes, he heard a man yelling for help. "He was clinging to a small clump of trees in the middle of the water," remembered Nicholson the following day from his hospital bed. "When I tried to help him, the current caught me. I was going downstream when I got on to the man's overturned car. I was on that car in the river for two and a half hours." When the river began to push the car downstream, Nicholson jumped into the water and managed to grab hold of a tree, where he sat for three more hours before rescuers could reach him. "I heard the sound of a fence being broken and saw the end of a truck backing toward the river. It was a fire truck and next I saw a great ladder going up in the air and over the river." Nicholson was pulled ashore, where rescuers doused him with rubbing alcohol. Jack Bates, the man Nicholson tried to help, was also in the torrent for hours until he was rescued: "Several times when I had water in my lungs and the trees were giving way I thought: 'This is it, I've had it.'"

Toronto Telegram/York University Archives 1754

Alex Nicholson, who had been directing cars away from flooded areas near his home on Pottery Road along the Don River, sat atop this car for two and a half hours awaiting rescue, then spent another three hours in a tree. Nicholson's story featured prominently in the media in the days following the storm.

The rivers and creeks that thread across the city provided the most serious threat to life, but Hazel dumped rain everywhere. Streets all over the city flooded into yards and through front doors and basement windows. Four-year-old Michael Campbell of Cosburn Avenue in East York nearly found himself listed among the casualties of the great storm. "I remember my mom and dad playing cards with my uncle Aldo by candlelight at the kitchen table. The basement stairs were off to one side. I had to go pee and got up, so they gave me a candle so I could go down into the basement. As I made my way down the stairs I burnt myself with the dripping wax. Somehow I slipped on the stairs and fell into water," Campbell says. "I remember trying to touch

HURRICANE HAZEL

Canada's Storm of the Century

Hazel's winds hovered around 70 miles per hour, but gusts of 100 miles per hour were reported. At the Toronto Island airport, the wind picked up this Cessna like a model airplane and flipped it upside down.

Les Baxter/Toronto Port Authority PC14/1203

Les Baxter/Toronto Port Authority PC14/1204

the bottom with my toes but it was over my head and I became very frightened. No one realized that the basement was flooded to within a few feet of the ceiling. It was very dark and I managed to catch hold of something, probably the stairs, while I cried out to my parents. They heard me and of course I was soon rescued."

In Oshawa, Warren Lanning, his son Bruce, and a family friend found themselves stranded in their car in the flood water, wrapping around a bridge. The three exited the car, walking away with ten-year-old Bruce on the friend's shoulders. The water surged, tearing Bruce off the man's shoulders and dragging him downstream. His body was later found miles away.

To the northeast of Toronto a CN train en route to Peterborough ploughed into a washout near Markham and derailed. The engineer and fireman leapt to safety just as the train lunged into the water. "We both saw the hole in the tracks ahead of us. We pulled the air brakes and jumped," recalled engineer Ted Barnett. Another train, on its return to Southampton, near Lake Huron, derailed as it neared the station. "The train toppled over on its side," passenger Bertha Whittaker later recalled. "The windows smashed. I was sitting there with the water running around me and blood running down my face." Whittaker survived, but Gordon McCallum, the engineer, and fireman Stewart Nicolson, who was injured when the train's boiler burst, would later become two more of Hazel's victims.

Hazel's fury reached farther north to fertile Holland Landing, where the de Peuter family, who had moved to Canada from Holland only five months before, had established a farm. The de Peuter house was lifted off its foundation poles and set adrift. For five hours Mr. and Mrs. Johann de Peuter and their twelve children scurried back and forth across their floating house to balance it as it began to tip over. The three youngest children became seasick. The house tore down hydro and tele-

In her fury, Hazel shoved this CN train off the tracks near Markham, Ontario, like a toy in a child's train set. The tracks lie twisted, steel rails bent as if by a giant's hand. No one was killed when this train hit a washout, but two members of a train's crew near Locust Hill along Lake Huron were not so lucky.

phone wires on its cruise before eventually landing a kilometre and a half from its original moorings. Bill de Peuter, a boy at the time and still a resident of the area today, will never forget Hazel. When Hurricane Isabel threatened southern Ontario in September 2003, de Peuter thought again of the 1954 storm that turned his house into a schooner. He told a reporter from the *Globe and Mail* that he didn't think his new house would float as well as the old one.

Two dikes holding back water in the Holland Marsh broke, forcing the evacuation of a number of families. One family, the Brands, had no choice but to drive through the worst of the storm to seek help for Anna Marie, their eleven-year-old daughter, who was suffering from pneumonia. North of Aurora, the car became stuck in the rising water. Famous Canadian wrestler Whipper Billy Watson and his friend Stewart Graham were on their way home from a fishing trip when they heard of the Brands' predicament. They quickly formed a rescue squad and took the family to nearby York County Hospital in Newmarket in their own cars.

The Holland Marsh became a bayou of onions, carrots, packing crates, and personal possessions. Flood water churned the fertile topsoil, covering it in a thick layer of silt and debris, damaging the soil and threatening the livelihood of thousands of farmers, many of whom had only just arrived in the country to set up new lives.

Archives of Ontario/RG 14 B-10-2 #423, 9

Lake Simcoe Region Conservation Authority

Lake Simcoe Region Conservation Authority

Newmarket and other outlying towns were inundated with water, damaging roads and hydro and telephone lines.

Even as many volunteers gave up their days and nights to search for those lost in the storm, the dark side of humanity showed its face. After three break-ins occurred in Oshawa at night after the power went out, police instructed storeowners via CFRB radio to park their cars in front of their shops to protect their interests. Police, Boy Scouts, and other volunteers patrolled the streets of Weston and Etobicoke, guarding against looters.

With dawn beginning to light up the city, rescuers and victims returned to their homes or to various shelters hastily set up to accommodate those who had lost everything.

Hazel moved on in the night, becoming a quieter, less destructive storm as it moved north to Timmins and out over James Bay. The rain no longer fell upon beleaguered southern Ontario. An estimated 280 millimetres of rain had fallen in less than 48 hours. Ninety percent of the rain that fell on the Humber River left as runoff. Nearly four thousand people were left homeless, and eighty-one were killed. In addition to the loss of life, Hazel caused $25 million in damage, the equivalent of around $150 million today.

The Sutton Co-op surrounded by water early Saturday morning, October 16, 1954.

Above left: *A billboard overlooking Lakeshore Road at the Humber warns motorists to "Drive Safely" as they approach the barrier blocking off the maw of the mangled bridge. Road crews worked steadily for weeks repairing or demolishing existing bridges, and the military erected Bailey bridges to allow stranded residents to traverse the city.*

Above right: *Even ten days after the storm, flotsam and jetsam that thundered down the Humber still lies scattered at the mouth of Lake Ontario near the Palace Pier, a popular dance hall.*

Left: *The waterline on this house is clearly visible, taller than the man in the photograph.*

J.V. Salmon/Toronto Public Library T33253

Toronto woke up a city in utter confusion. Cars sat embedded in the mud next to the Humber River, which had become an immense, mucky parking lot. Several streetcars stood on their sides like toy trains tossed into a massive brown bathtub. In the trees hung clothes, tires, appliances, dolls, umbrellas, windows, personal papers, records, even dead cows and pigs.

Top Left: *This bridge, along the McDonald-Cartier Freeway west of Albion Road, had just been completed at a cost of $225,000 when Hazel hit. The bridge was too damaged to attempt repairs and was dynamited in November 1954.*

Bottom left and below: *Hazel plucked these TTC streetcars, weighing several tons each, from their sidings and deposited them in the Humber.*

Toronto and Region Conservation Authority

Toronto and Region Conservation Authority

Ross Grinnell/Archives of Ontario/RG 1-488-1 Box 9

Martin Taylor

Ted Chirnside/Toronto Public Library TC0006

Above left and right: *For days after the storm, cars such as these near Fair Glen Crescent sat in the Humber up to their wheel wells.*

Left: *Hazel swiped at the sides of these houses at Hogg's Hollow overlooking the Don River. Several houses were later torn down. Across from where these houses once stood, on the west side of Yonge Street, north of York Mills, a city golf course now reaches north under the 401, touching on a steep embankment at the south end of Lansing.*

Many had gone to bed unaware of the horrific events that would unfold during the night, only to find the world turned on its head when they awoke.

To many, especially children, Hazel had turned Toronto into a new and exciting world. Roman Tarnovetsky was a seven-year-old boy living in the poor Ukrainian neighbourhood of Dundas and Ossington when Hazel hit. "Our parents were buzzing when we

Left: *Children enjoying a snack beside road damage near York Mills Road and Bayview Avenue the day after the storm.*

Below: *Everyday items like washing machines, bicycles, clothes, dishes, furniture, and toys littered the areas surrounding the rivers and creeks of Weston, Etobicoke, Toronto, and Scarborough. For weeks after the storm, Marj Mossman and her friends would find bike pedals and other items jutting out of the ground.*

Ross Grinnell/Archives of Ontario/RG 1-448-1 Box 9

Toronto and Region Conservation Authority

went to bed, and when we woke up it was like Christmas. We wanted to see if the world was still there, and it was. Saturday, October 16, was a day of reverberation. We heard stories. There were few radios and only one television in the neighbourhood. We watched the reports of the storm," he says. "My father treated us to a streetcar ride to the end of the Queen line near Roncesvalles, where we looked at the damage. It was an extravagance, the entire family riding the streetcar at once. I felt the anxiety of everyone around and knew that something significant was happening, but it was exciting for a child of my age."

Marj Mossman, then in her early teens, also remembers having a sense of wonder. "Chickens stayed around the neighbourhood for weeks, living in everyone's woodpiles. The birds must have floated down the river. I don't know what happened to them later," she recalls. "The water lasted for days. The Humber Valley looked so beautiful a few days after the storm. The leaves were all yellow, the red sumacs were in full bloom. But even with all that beauty, we knew what had happened, that everything wasn't back to normal. It was very deceiving."

Toronto and Region Conservation Authority

Daylight on October 16 revealed a magical world for children. Here a lifesaver from the pool of the Rouge Valley Inn in Scarborough lies upon the buckled cement and battered exterior of what was once Funland.

O N THE NIGHT OF THE STORM THE CITY'S Boy Scout troops and their leaders had holed up in churches and assembly halls around the city polishing apples for the next day's annual Apple Day. "My Scouts and I were at St. John's Presbyterian Church in the Broadview and Gerrard area, polishing apples. We went home in the rain and thought it was just a bad rainstorm. I woke up the next day to find out that it wasn't," remembers Don Boyd. "On Monday I took a day off work and the Scouts took a day off school and we went out to the Bloor and Dundas area to help search for bodies in the Humber Valley. We started off at Bloor Street and walked down to Lake Ontario. We saw lots of destruction — refrigerators and huge timbers from barns in trees. Thank goodness we didn't find any bodies."

Looking west across the Old Albion Bridge over the Humber River. Dozens of bridges were washed out or damaged beyond repair.

Twenty-four-year-old Harry Bruce was a Rover, a young adult Scout dedicated to public service. He had heard about Hazel's destruction but, like many, did not think that it was anything worse than a bad thunderstorm. It wasn't until Saturday afternoon, when he and other Scouts were counting the proceeds of their apple sales, that they saw the headlines and realized what had happened. "On Sunday a bunch of us went out to a fire hall in Etobicoke to volunteer. The hall was being used as a makeshift morgue. We searched for bodies in an area where they had found bodies the day before. We were thankful that we didn't find any." After trudging through the Humber River Valley for the morning, Bruce and his friends returned to the fire hall for a box lunch, which they ate near the bodies of several victims of the storm.

Glen Gibbs was summoned by his high school cadet group on October 17 to search for bodies in the Humber Valley. He was overcome by grief at the sight of the loss of life and could not continue in the search.

This sign, posted near the Don River at Bathurst Street north of Sheppard Avenue in North York, understates the looming danger. Late on Friday, October 15, several motorists, blinded by the pounding rain, drove into rivers, unaware that the bridges had been washed away.

Toronto Public Library HS37

Weston Historical Society

Above left: *Local women provide sandwiches, coffee, and good cheer for volunteers in Humber Summit.*

Above right, and left: *Wayne Plunkett, then a thirteen-year-old living in Weston, clearly remembers the aftermath of Hazel: "I walked down to the Humber River at about eight in the morning to see what was going on. I was grabbed by the scruff of the neck and was not-so-politely asked if I knew what I was going to be doing for the rest of the day. 'What's that?' I asked. 'Sandbagging the Weston Arena. Do you play hockey? Do you want to keep the arena? Then you'd better get sandbagging. If we don't get this sandbagged, the arena's going to go down the river.' All morning I helped, till about noon when we ran out of bags."*

Firefighters Don "Red" Leslie and Byard Donnelly of No. 2 Fire Hall in North York, at Lawrence Avenue and Bathurst Street, gave their days off to help search for victims of the storm. "There was debris in the trees," recalls Leslie. "There was a rubber plant in Bolton at the time that made prophylactics. The trees were full of the things, fifteen feet up, hanging from the trees like balloons. I was only twenty-three at the time. I didn't know anything about them."

Richard Sargent/Byard Donnelly

The Humber Summit crew in the days following the hurricane. Back row (l-r): unknown volunteer, Don "Red" Leslie, Frank Purvis, George Marshall, Neil McNamara, Jim Murray, Denny Hammond, Les Pratt, Val Delory, and Dave Hyndeman. Front row (l-r): Eric Parkes, Bill McDonald, Byard Donnelly, Alex Baird, Wells Pehlman, Tommy Thompson, Bill Stanfield, Art Serle, John (Toby) Taylor, Frank Bennet, Roy Floyd, and Bob Rogers.

Donnelly also remembers the "safes" hanging in the trees. "Furniture, buildings, stoves — there was stuff all over the place," he says. "We worked out of the Humber Summit volunteer hall looking for bodies. We found a small child, a boy of eight or nine, in Woodbridge. It was the only body we ever found. Bodies went right down the river into the lake." For Donnelly, who had served aboard the frigate HMCS *Runnymede* on convoy duty in the North Atlantic during the Second World War, the experience was not as daunting as he thought it might be. "I joined the navy at seventeen and grew up quick. To me, after seeing what I had seen at sea, Hazel wasn't that big of a disaster. I knew it was bad, but I didn't get upset because I had seen worse."

Two men atop a train bridge near Lakeshore Road watch as two other men salvage boats from the remains of Barton's Boat House, flattened by debris caught in the torrential runoff.

Wallace Rombough and Malcolm Cliff, who had spent much of the night rescuing people in a small boat, returned to the Humber after a few hours of sleep and took to the air in a Harvard Trainer, intent on finding bodies in the valley, but they were unsuccessful. Later in the day Rombough visited Ward's Funeral Home in Weston, where he witnessed the mud and silt being hosed off some of Hazel's victims.

The Canadian military, again a peacetime entity after the conclusion of the Korean War only one year before, returned to action. Around two thousand airmen from the RCAF conducted air and ground searches. A search and rescue centre was set up at Downsview. Civilian and military helicopters hovered over the Humber River, from

This outbuilding was flipped on its side and became embedded in the mud.

Ted Grant/National Archives of Canada/E002107668

Bloor Street north to Woodbridge, looking for survivors. The army, including the 18th Field Squadron out of Hamilton, sent one hundred men to detonate the remains of bridges around the city with the assistance of personnel flown in from Chilliwack, British Columbia. Army personnel erected Bailey bridges at critical junctures, allowing traffic to flow between boroughs isolated after the flooding washed away approaches.

Gordon Jolley/National Archives of Canada/PA-174538

Gordon Jolley/National Archives of Canada/PA-174539

Gordon Jolley/National Archives of Canada/PA-174540

Gordon Jolley/National Archives of Canada/PA-174541

The army clearing away debris after the storm. Regiments from across Canada descended upon the west end of Toronto to search for bodies, pump out swamped land, and remove trees, houses, and other items that blocked rivers and creeks. They burned what they could not salvage.

Toronto and Region Conservation Authority

A helicopter, a mere speck on a canvas of flooded farmland, hovers over Woodbridge. Military and civilian helicopters surveyed the Humber from Woodbridge south to Lake Ontario, directing workers on the ground.

HURRICANE HAZEL
Canada's Storm of the Century

J.V. Salmon/Toronto Public Library T33239

Left: *A Woodbridge resident has mounted a ladder up the side of his house, which has been torn from its foundations. Even after the snow fell in December, this house still rested crookedly against a tree.*

Below left: *The 48th Highlanders search for bodies on the Humber River south of the Dundas Street bridge.*

Below right: *Flames shoot out of a Wasp, a flame-throwing Bren gun carrier, burning away debris collected by the army.*

Archives of Ontario/10013856

Archives of Ontario/10013853

In late October, militia units participated in Operation Search II, a two-day sweep along the Humber River, looking for those still counted among the missing, especially where Raymore Drive had once been. From headquarters inside the main entrance of the Lambton Golf Course, regiments including the Toronto Scottish 48th Highlanders, Irish Regiment of Canada, Lorne Scots, 2nd Field Engineering, 2nd Signals, 2nd Medical Training Battalion, and Royal Regiment of Canada marched through the muck as anguished families awaited word.

Ken Bell/National Archives of Canada/E002107886

Ken Bell, a military photographer best known for his photos of the Canadian landing at Juno Beach on June 6, 1944, captured this and several other images of the Canadian army helping out on the home front. Here, a Bren gun carrier with the Royal Regiment of Canada rolls into Weston around what used to be Raymore Drive. On October 30 and 31, 1954, several regiments searched for bodies, burned brush, and helped locals uncover their belongings.

HURRICANE HAZEL
Canada's Storm of the Century

Members of the Royal Regiment appear almost casual as they nudge the bottom of a shallow area looking for bodies, two weeks after Hazel devastated Toronto's west end.

Ken Bell/National Archives of Canada/E002107884

78

What was once an outbuilding lies crumpled and broken, the only thing left standing as the army gathers chairs, timbers, cooking utensils, and other items from a family home.

Ken Bell/National Archives of Canada/E002107867

79

A woman points to what might have been her home as an army officer checks his paperwork and locals examine the damage.

80

Building a bonfire. The army collected timbers and boards torn from houses in Weston.

Ken Bell/National Archives of Canada/E002107888

81

HURRICANE HAZEL
Canada's Storm of the Century

A civilian bulldozes broken concrete and dirt. Flood water from the Humber, several feet high, wrenched walls off houses, stripping them down to cinder blocks.

Ken Bell/National Archives of Canada/E002107871

82

The Royal Regiment takes a break from search operations. In full uniform and hip waders, the soldiers crack open refreshments.

Ken Bell/National Archives of Canada/E002107865

As they often do during desperate times, the Red Cross and the Salvation Army offered their full assistance in recovery efforts. Both organizations solicited donations for the Hurricane Relief Fund, and would continue to do so far into the new year. The Red Cross found itself helping out those at home instead of those abroad and published ads petitioning Canadians for funds. One read, "When Hurricane Hazel struck with sledgehammer fury your Red Cross was ready. This is the Red Cross in action … in Canada." Another, "Disaster can happen here. You are serving in any emergency when you give to the Red Cross." Mobile canteens circled flood-stricken areas, offering blankets, food, and clothing to victims and rescuers.

The Salvation Army accepts donations for the Hurricane Hazel Relief Fund on Yonge Street. They, along with the Red Cross, fed and comforted storm victims and consoled mourning family members at makeshift morgues and funerals.

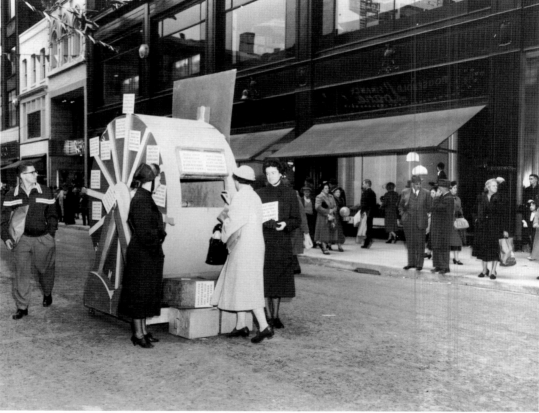

Roy Mitchell/National Archives of Canada/RD931

Salvation Army donation bubbles (bottom right) are a regular fixture at street corners and malls during the Christmas shopping frenzy, but made for an unusual sight at Halloween 1954. This volunteer has selected a prime location south of Gerrard Street on Yonge, at the time a pedestrian mall. The Salvation Army collected $14,000 in one day.

Roy Mitchell/National Archives of Canada/RD00929

It so happened that the weekend Hazel struck the city, the Salvation Army's "congress weekend" was underway in Toronto. Hundreds of officers were in Toronto for a meeting of the organization's international leaders. As the bodies of the flood's victims found their way to various makeshift morgues, officers comforted families who had come to identify their loved ones. The Salvation Army coordinated relief efforts out of the armouries on University Avenue to sort out clothing and other necessities. Volunteers could scarcely keep up with deliveries of donated clothing. Major D. Strachan was under orders to close the depot at nine-thirty, but at midnight people were still emptying their closets and venturing down to the armouries. As the clothing piles mounted beyond control, a man phoned the depot offering his truck to drive two tons of supplies to the Holland Marsh. Later, a convoy of twenty-eight trucks, including eight tractor-trailers, hauled supplies from the armouries to the Holland Marsh. A truckload of supplies arrived from Flint, Michigan. A man from Ann Arbor, Michigan, trucked in twenty-five tons of supplies. The Salvation

City of Toronto Archives, series 6, item 242

Metro Toronto Department of Works collects and burns mountains of wood during the winter, under pressure to clear the rivers before they flooded again in the spring.

Army in Buffalo, New York, shipped a mobile canteen, complete with two personnel who volunteered their services for several days.

The Salvation Army sent out cadets along Yonge Street, which was at the time a street mall closed to automobile traffic, to set up the donation "bubbles" found on many street corners at Christmas — an unusual sight at Halloween. Men and women in full Salvation Army regalia rang bells and politely asked Torontonians to dig deeper to help out the victims of the hurricane.

Pledges of cash donations came in from around Toronto and across the country. The Ford Motor Company made a $25,000 donation before the Hurricane Relief Fund was even established. CHCH-TV in Hamilton pledged $57,000 for the victims of the disaster. Toronto City Council voted for a donation of $50,000. Major cash

Ted Grant/National Archives of Canada/E002107664

In the aftermath of the storm, cars sat embedded in the muck of ditches, rivers, even front yards. Many vehicles, silt up to the steering wheel, were undriveable and sat as rotting husks until cleanup crews arrived to pull them out of the ground.

Toronto and Region Conservation Authority

HURRICANE HAZEL
Canada's Storm of the Century

Even on October 16, water still surged over the Humber's embankments south of Old Dundas Street. Less than twenty-four hours before, these onlookers would have been washed down the Humber and out into Lake Ontario had they dared stand so close to the torrent.

donations rolled in from companies such as Algoma Steel Corp., Canada Steamship Lines, Consumers' Glass Co. Ltd., Laura Secord, and John Labatt. The United Church of Canada and the Kinsman Clubs of Canada each offered sizeable donations for the cause. The mayor of Windsor anted up $500 to inspire Windsor residents to pry open their wallets. The city of Winnipeg, the victim of a memorable flood only a few years before, asked its citizens to reciprocate the goodwill the city had received during its own difficult times. J.E. Houck of Brampton auctioned a Holstein heifer newly

named "Flood Relief." The cow was sold then put back up for auction fifteen times, raising $2,000 for the relief fund. Brigham Young University in Utah won the final bid, paying $385 for the popular bovine.

To many, the big storm was nothing more than a big nuisance. The storm knocked twenty bridges out of action and closed down several roads. "I worked at A.V. Rowe on the Orenda engines for the CF-100 aircraft," recalls Neil Walker. "Saturday was overtime for me. We usually took the Dundas Street bridge to get there, but it was blocked off. We went up to Highway 7 in Woodbridge. We saw a house sticking out in the air at an awkward angle. We went farther up, past Pine Grove, driving around trying to find a way to get to work. I ended up being two hours late."

The other Hurricane Hazel, Mississauga Mayor Hazel McCallion, long recognized as a force of her own, remembers the storm as an inconvenience. "We lived in Streetsville on Britannia at the time," she says. "The night of the storm I went to bed. The next morning the hydro was out, trees were knocked down, debris was piled up. We wandered the streets looking for a way to get around the trees lying across all the roads. Police stood on street corners guiding traffic, but it was a mess."

Even the cinder-block foundation of this house could not withstand the millions of gallons of water that exploded over riverbanks from Woodbridge south to Long Branch.

Ted Grant/National Archives of Canada/E002107669

S WITH ANY DISASTER, WITHIN A FEW DAYS life began returning to normal, except for those who had lost their homes or families as a result of the storm. Now began the battles with insurance companies and banks. Many had to begin all over again.

Sound vans drove down residential streets warning people to boil their water, which might have become contaminated. The city erected warning signs on houses decimated by flooding, now unfit for human habitation. Off Long Branch Avenue, flood water cut a path through six months' worth of garbage the city had permitted to be dumped in a nearby creek. Hundreds of rats fled the destruction of their home for the basements of Long Branch residents.

Insurance agents in Ontario spent thousands of hours sorting through paperwork after Hazel smashed houses, businesses, and cars. Insurance companies today fear the arrival of another Hazel-sized event in the Greater Toronto Area. Basements once used as storage areas now feature home theatres and furnished apartments.

Gordon W. Powley/Archives of Ontario/C 5-2-2-33-4/1002915

Ted Grant/National Archives of Canada/E002107657

Bill Dixon

243

OUT OF BOUNDS
TO
UNAUTHORIZED PERSONS
AND
NON-RESIDENTS • POLICE OFFICER

CONDEMNED
UNIT FOR
HUMAN
HABITATION

Above: *Bill Dixon, who piloted Lancaster and Wellington bombers during the Second World War, moved into his new home near Mimico Creek only days before that fateful Friday. Immobilized by a broken back from an automobile accident, Dixon watched helplessly as the storm washed away much of his new property.*

Left: *The Medical Officer of Health forced many residents to leave their homes until "put in proper sanitary condition."*

In Hogg's Hollow, once-grand houses hung precariously over Yonge Street south of York Mills awaiting demolition. A Bailey bridge constructed by the military over the Don provided the only north-south access for miles.

In addition to its human toll, Hazel wiped out livestock and other animals. Witnesses reported sightings of pigs and cows hanging in the trees of the northern reaches of the Humber like the living realization of a Salvador Dali painting. In Bradford, 150 head of cattle went missing. Winds knocked down chicken coops, swept up the birds, and sent them into the river. Frank Coleman lost

J.V. Salmon/Toronto Public Library T33266

Toronto and Region Conservation Authority

Above left and right: *The bridge over the Don River at Hogg's Hollow was irreparably damaged. The military erected a Bailey bridge to allow north-south traffic to flow along Yonge Street south of York Mills Road.*

Right: *Volunteers launch a boat to search the receding river. Curious locals, unused to such sights, watch on.*

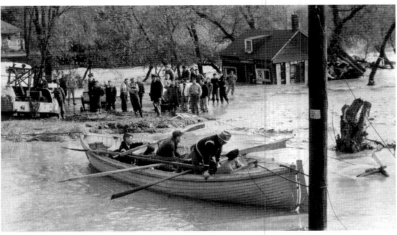

Toronto and Region Conservation Authority

$15,000 worth of mink at his farm in Newmarket. At the Sunnybrook Stables, a group of fifteen senior Boy Scouts volunteered to herd forty horses through three feet of water. The storm wiped out flocks of pheasant, effectively ending the hunting season, especially in Brampton. Hunters and hikers found dozens of the dead birds. "The few remaining have made scarce hunting for nimrods beating the area in the four-day season," reported the *Globe and Mail*. Hunters pleaded with authorities to release a minimum of five hundred more birds into the wild so they could continue with the hunt.

Some victims of the storm became virtual refugees on their own land. Some of the Woodbridge residents who had fled their crushed trailers found temporary housing on the Woodbridge Fairgrounds, signing leases allowing them to remain on the land until June 1955. One resident, a widower with five children, paid $45 a month for

Right: *Hazel took more than its human toll. Dead cows, pigs, dogs, chickens, and other animals washed down rivers and hung from trees. Liberated livestock ran down residential streets. In this photo, the remains of a chicken coop.*

Below left and right: *The Department of Works ushered in heavy road equipment to bulldoze the unfathomable damage.*

Ted Grant/National Archives of Canada/E002107673

Ted Chirnside/Toronto Public Library TC0106A

Archives of Ontario/10013858

These houses, near Riverside Drive in Humber Summit, were so damaged by the storm that you could no longer read the addresses, which have been painted on the exterior walls. This settlement resembled a war zone in the aftermath of Hazel.

temporary housing, plus $63 a week for meals. As late as February 1955, forty families still called the makeshift housing their home.

In Bradford, the Canadian National Railways station was opened up as a relief depot, offering food and drink for the workers building up dikes to contain the flood water. CNR offered several Pullman cars as temporary housing for refugees of the devastation in the Holland Landing area.

Day by day, people rebuilt their lives and moved on. The Humber resumed its course, a much quieter river than it had been at the peak of Hazel. The Don

Jim Gifford

Above: *"Last Alarm." Etched among the names of lost fire-fighters on this monument on Queens Quay are the names of the five Kingsway-Lambton firefighters lost during Hurricane Hazel.*

Right: *Just south of Bloor and Dundas streets in the west end sits this monument to the five lost volunteer firefighters. The original memorial, made out of the materials of the lost truck, stood for years in a park at Prince Edward Drive and Marquis Avenue, until it was stolen in 1980.*

Jim Gifford

receded as well, allowing normal traffic to resume in North Toronto. Road crews repaired damaged shoulders and cracked asphalt. Teams of city workers and army personnel ventured into river valleys to dig out and burn the tangle of trees and just about everything else that interrupted the flow of

95

the water. Humber Heights School on Lawrence Avenue, which had assumed duty as a morgue, a health unit, and an emergency fire station following the storm, once again became only a school. People pumped out their basements, cleared storm drains, rebuilt fences, and fixed what they could before winter set in.

Left: *Humber Heights School became a hospital, health unit, and makeshift morgue in the days after the hurricane. "A few days after the storm I went to Humber Heights to get a typhoid shot," remembers Dave Iris. "I still have the scar."*

Above: *Still in shock from the unlikely arrival of a northern hurricane, residents wade through a maze of flattened houses, rescuing what they can. Thousands were left homeless after the storm and found shelter in trailers, motels, and arenas until they could arrange their affairs.*

This plaque, affixed to a stone in Marie Curtis Park, memorializes the lost and commemorates the brave rescuers who risked their own lives to save others in the early hours of October 16, 1954.

Jim Gifford

I N THE YEARS FOLLOWING HURRICANE HAZEL, THE CITY of Toronto and the province of Ontario opened up discussions about the creation of a new body that would ensure that the devastation caused by the great storm of 1954 would be unlikely to recur. The Metropolitan Toronto and Region Conservation Authority (MTRCA), later the Toronto Regional Conservation Authority (TRCA), was born out of the rubble of the hurricane. In 1959, the new authority published a report recommending under its governance "a series of dams and reservoirs to

HURRICANE HAZEL
Canada's Storm of the Century

One of several parks created in the wake of Hurricane Hazel, Marie Curtis Park in Long Branch is now a green area, host to cyclists, picnickers, and hikers. Fifty years ago seven people were killed in a nearby cottage settlement.

impound flood waters, the improvement of stream channels at critical points to facilitate the operation of the dams and reservoirs, and the acquisition of certain tracts of vulnerable flood plain." The authority offered a complex formula for calculating the value of land and property versus the value of loss of human life. "Survival, cultural, and aesthetic values are inadequately measured by price. It could, for instance, be considered immoral as well as absurd to presume to measure the value of a human life. But a human life does have an economic worth as a factor of production or as an insurable entity." The MTRCA suggested that "the value of the net benefits of flood plain land used for conservation and parks would be at least equal to the acquisition cost of the land." Since its inception, the authority has appropriated more than twenty-six thousand acres of land in the city's various floodplains (especially in the Humber Valley, where a recurrence during a similar storm is most likely) and has turned it into parkland, complete with bike and hiking trails. Where houses and cottages once lined a quiet but lurking danger, now only grass and pathways lie in the path of future disaster.

"The city has a unique fabric, with green fingers going throughout the city, because of Hurricane Hazel. We couldn't buy the world, but we needed to keep people safe," says Don Haley, a water resources engineer with the TRCA. "We figured out where the floodplains were and said that no new homes, nothing, could be built there. The land was turned into golf courses and parks or was used for agriculture. Hurricane Hazel was a key factor in the greening of the city. It provided a vehicle to make things happen. New York City has one big park, but Toronto is very green all over."

Jim Gifford

Where Raymore Drive once was now sits Raymore Park, as well as a new footbridge over the Humber dedicated to the thirty-two Raymore residents lost in October 1954.

Jim Gifford

The families of those eighty-one people who lost their lives during the night of October 15, 1954, will find that of little solace, but thousands are no longer in the direct path of the surging Humber or Don rivers. Today, people cycle and rollerblade where fifty years ago the river swelled beyond its banks and pulled unsuspecting victims into its depths.

Could it happen again? Could a storm like Hazel again submerge Toronto? For all of the planning to avoid such an eventuality, anything can happen. The insurance companies fear the worst. Since 1954 the city has grown exponentially. Basements once used for storage now house media rooms complete with televisions, stereos, and DVD players. The cost of damage caused by basement flooding after an event such as Hazel could exceed $400 million. It would be extremely difficult to predict the loss of property and life should another Hazel-size storm hit the city, but the Toronto and regional conservation authorities have worked hard to protect a city with only a simmering memory of the disaster of 1954.

When Hurricane Isabel threatened Toronto in September 2003, the newspapers warned of imminent danger a week before it arrived, but Isabel dissipated long before she could match Hazel's fury; inside-out umbrellas and broken branches were her worst offences. A headline in the *National Post* suggested, "Go to work today, Isabel can't make it." Hurricane Juan, a much less heralded storm (that is, it landed nowhere near Toronto), devastated the East Coast only a month later, dunking boats, damaging buildings and piers, and flipping mobile homes along the shores of Nova Scotia.

We now lead insulated lives, free of much of the danger that threatened Toronto, a city unprepared, in 1954. We seem to beg for danger. "People thought they'd be hunkered down for a couple of weeks. They'd gone out and bought milk and bread and toilet paper," reported Dave Phillips, senior climatologist at Environment Canada, after Isabel disappointed the city. "Let's face it, people like to see human misery and there hasn't been anyone floating down the Humber River."

There is a one in a hundred chance that a storm as fierce as Hazel will hit Toronto in any given year. Today every time the swirling, misty, milky form of a hurricane shows up on a satellite weather map, those who recall Hazel watch it carefully, remembering those desperate, dark hours on an October night in 1954, when a city came together.

BIBLIOGRAPHY

Books

Barnes, Jay. *North Carolina's Hurricane History*. 3rd ed. Chapel Hill, NC: University of North Carolina Press, 2001.

Davies, Pete. *Inside the Hurricane: Face to Face with Nature's Deadliest Storms*. New York: Henry Holt and Company, 2000.

Dunn, Gordon E., and Banner I. Miller. *Atlantic Hurricanes*. Baton Rouge, LA: Louisiana State University Press, 1960.

Filey, Mike. *A Toronto Album 2: More Glimpses of the City That Was*. Toronto: Dundurn Press, 2002.

Filey, Mike. *Toronto Sketches 4: The Way We Were*. Toronto: Dundurn Press, 1995.

Institute for Catastrophic Loss Reduction. *Hurricane Hazel and Extreme Rainfall in Southern Ontario*, ICLR Research Paper Series, No. 9. Toronto: Cumming Cockburn Limited, November 2000.

Kennedy, Betty. *Hurricane Hazel*. Toronto: Macmillan of Canada, 1979.

Kirkpatrick, Robert B. *Their Last Alarm: Honouring Ontario's Firefighters*. Burnstown, Ontario: General Store Publishing House, 2002.

Larson, Erik. *Isaac's Storm: A Man, a Time, and the Deadliest Hurricane in History*. Toronto: Vintage Books, 1999.

Lemon, James. *Toronto Since 1918: An Illustrated History*. The History of Canadian Cities series. Toronto: James Lorimer & Company/National Museum of Man, 1985.

Long, Megan. *Disaster Great Lakes*. Toronto: Lynx Images, Inc., 2002.

Looker, Janet. *Disaster Canada*. Toronto: Lynx Images, Inc., 2000.

Metropolitan Toronto and Region Conservation Authority. *Plan for Flood Control and Water Conservation*. Woodbridge, Ontario: MTRCA, 1959.

Sheets, Dr. Bob, and Jack Williams. *Hurricane Watch: Forecasting the Deadliest Storms on Earth*. Toronto: Vintage Books, 2001.

Video

Disasters of the Century: Nature's Fury (episode 2), Partners in Motion, in association with History Television, Saskatchewan Communications Network, and Harmony Entertainment Management Inc., 2000.

Web Sites

CBC Archives http://archives.cbc.ca

Canadian Hurricane Centre http://www.ns.ec.gc.ca/weather/hurricane/index_e.html

Disasters HQ http://www.disastershq.com/features/hazel.asp

Environment Canada http://www.ns.ec.gc.ca/weather/hurricane/storm54.html

Martin Taylor http://www.mmtaylor.net/History/Hurricane_Hazel/